ANGUS - CULTURAL SERVICES

3 8046 00656

Leavi
the Island

D0186726

ARBROATH This book is to be returned on or
before the last date stamped below.

2 0 OCT 1999

2 0 DEC 1999

-9 MAY 2000 ANGUSalive

-6 DEC 2003

Withdrawn from stock

-2 AUG 2004

25 AUG 2005

1 4 AUG 2006

1 5 SEP 2008

1 1 NOV 2009

1 1 MAR 2016

Angus Council

CULTURAL SERVICES

FW SEP 1998

JUNIOR

Cambridge Reading

General Editors
Richard Brown and Kate Ruttle

Consultant Editor
Jean Glasberg

PUBLISHED BY THE PRESS SYNDICATE OF THE UNIVERSITY OF CAMBRIDGE
The Pitt Building, Trumpington Street, Cambridge CB2 1RP, United Kingdom

CAMBRIDGE UNIVERSITY PRESS
The Edinburgh Building, Cambridge CB2 2RU, United Kingdom
40 West 20th Street, New York, NY 10011-4211, USA
10 Stamford Road, Oakleigh, Melbourne 3166, Australia

Leaving the Island
Text © Judith O'Neill 1998
Text illustrations © Lisa Kopper 1998
Cover illustration © James Bartholomew 1998

This book is in copyright. Subject to statutory exception and to the provisions
of relevant collective licensing agreements, no reproduction of any part may
take place without the written permission of Cambridge University Press.

First published 1998

Printed in the United Kingdom by the University Press, Cambridge

Typeset in Concorde

A catalogue record for this book is available from the British Library

ISBN 0 521 63745 7 paperback

**Other Cambridge Reading books
you may enjoy**

Leopard on the Mountain
Ruskin Bond

The Midnight Party
Richard Brown

Never Meddle with Magic Mirrors!
Kaye Umansky

Clyde's Leopard
Helen Dunmore

**Other books by Judith O'Neill
you may enjoy**

Sharp Eyes

So Far from Skye

Hearing Voices

Right on Philip's tenth birthday, the letter
came. The letter they had all been dreading.
Dad tore it open. First his eyes skimmed the
typewritten sheet. Then he looked up at the
whole family where they sat in a circle around
Philip's cake and its ten blazing candles.

"We're leaving the island," he said, in a dull, flat voice.

"When?" asked Mum, suddenly pale.

"At the end of this month. Just in time for the children to start their new school year." Dad was trying to sound cheerful but he didn't succeed.

Ellie burst into tears. She howled. She was only six, after all.

"I won't go!" Anna shouted. She was the eldest.

Philip said nothing. He sat very still and fixed his eyes on the ten wavering candle flames. He was sure that this was the last *happy* birthday he would ever have in his whole life. Even this birthday was ruined now.

"Blow them out, Philip!" sobbed Ellie as the flames burned down to the icing.

Philip blew. His ten candles went out with one sad breath.

"We'll just have to make the best of it," Dad said brightly as Mum started cutting the cake. "We've had a good run here, haven't we? Six happy years. But now it's time to move to the next place. There's no choice, I'm afraid. I have to go where I'm sent. That's part of the job."

"But we don't have to go with you, Dad!" Anna protested. "We could stay here. You could go by yourself!"

Dad shook his head.

"You *do* all have to come with me, Anna. You know that. This house goes with the job. The next family is waiting to move in. *Our* next house is waiting for us in the city. You'll love the next house."

"We won't!" bellowed Ellie.

"You haven't said anything yet, Philip," Mum said, smiling anxiously at him over the remains of the cake. "What do *you* think?"

Philip took a long time to answer.

"I can't leave the island," he said at last.
"We belong here. Couldn't we just build a hut
on the beach and live there?"

Dad shook his head.

The cake tasted dry in Philip's mouth.

"Take Jip for his run on the beach, son,"
Dad said. "Let the wind blow your sadness
away."

Out on the beach, Philip ran fast with Jip by his side. For years he'd been running his dog along this clean, white sand. He and Jip knew every hollow in the dunes, every clump of grass, every long line of shells and seaweed where the waves turned back. He always told Jip the name of every bird that skimmed over the water. Jip always seemed to understand.

"I can't go! I can't go!" Philip mumbled to himself. He watched the waves rolling in,

dark green as they rose, white as they broke.
He listened as they hissed to the shore. That
hiss had always seemed friendly to Philip but
today it sounded mournful.

"You'll have to go! You'll have to
go!" the waves seemed to say.

"You'll never come back! You'll
never come back!" the gulls and
terns and kittiwakes seemed
to shriek overhead.

Philip and his family did have to go. Anna
kept protesting until the very last moment
when the furniture had been carried out to a
waiting van and the luggage was stowed in

the car. Dad drove over the causeway to the ferry on South Uist. The family stood in the stern of the ship and watched the islands grow smaller and smaller. Jip gave a wet snuffle.

"He's crying!" said Mum, blinking her own eyes hard.

Philip crouched down on the deck and looked right into Jip's eyes. Real tears were running down the dog's brown nose.

"He *is* crying!" gasped Philip in amazement. "He knows we'll never be back."

"Perhaps, one day," said Dad, but no-one was listening. Philip could only hear the wild cry of the sea-birds.

"You'll never come back! You'll never come back!"

Once they had reached the mainland, the journey was still long. They drove for hours until, at last, they reached the outskirts of the city. Cars snarled behind them and beside them. Buses scooped up waiting passengers and spewed others out onto the footpath. The noise of traffic rang loudly in Philip's ears. He could hardly remember the sound of the sea.

"Where's our new house?" Anna asked suspiciously, turning her head to look left and right.

"Not far now. We'll go past your school and then our house is just round the next corner," said Dad.

Philip gazed up at the school. It looked to him like a grim fortress. Grey stone and red brick, planted right in the centre of a black, asphalt yard.

"That's not a school, Dad!" he said indignantly. "That's a jail!"

"A school," Dad insisted. "*Your* school, Philip! And Anna's and Ellie's. It's one of the best schools in the city. Everyone says so."

Philip was silent. He kept thinking of his
old school on the island. It stood so close to
the sea that sometimes green waves came right
up to the door. He thought of his teacher, kind
Mrs Macmillan, and of his friends in her class.
He thought of the singing and the stories.
He thought of the shaky buses that brought
some children along bumpy roads every
morning and took them safely home again at
the end of the day. That island school was the
best school in the whole world, Philip was
thinking. It was nothing like a jail.

They camped in the empty, echoing house that night. The furniture came early the next morning. Everything looked strange in the new house. Jip moped in a corner.

"Take him for a run, Philip," said Dad. "But keep him on the lead. Just to the end of our street and back again. Don't let him dart into the traffic."

Philip nodded. Jip hated the lead. He pulled his head this way and that, trying to shake it off, but Philip held firm. They walked side by side to the end of the street, Jip pulling and Philip gripping hard. They turned and came back again.

"Is that all?" Jip seemed to be saying, looking up at Philip with puzzled eyes.

"That's it," said Philip.

School began the next day. Ellie was crying again. Anna was angry. Philip was silent. Mum led each of them in turn to the right classroom.

"This is Philip," she said, pushing him gently through the door.

The teacher was nothing like Mrs Macmillan, but he smiled down at Philip. "I'll put you next to Jim," he said. "He's new too."

"Do you come from an island?" Philip whispered to Jim. The boy shook his head.

"I come from another city," he whispered back. "It's much bigger than this one. Bigger and better. I didn't want to come here at all."

"Neither did I!" murmured Philip.

"Right now, everyone," said the teacher, briskly. "Settle down." The school day had begun.

As Philip was shuffling home that afternoon, just as he turned the corner and came to his own front gate, he was startled by a wailing, yelping sound, like a sick puppy.

"Kee-yow! Kee-yow!"

He caught sight of something white and grey and black, something flopping and flapping, something sobbing and crying on his very own doorstep. He ran to look.

Then he saw it, plain as day. It wasn't a puppy. A sea-bird lay there on her side, struggling and crying. She had white feathers, a silver-grey mantle, black tips on her wings. She had pink legs, a yellow bill and a bright, yellow eye.

"A herring gull!" cried Philip in surprise. "What are *you* doing here? You should be safe at home on your island, not lying all bent and broken in the middle of the city! Whatever's the matter with you?"

The bird fixed Philip with her yellow eye.

"Kee-yow," she cried. She shivered and trembled. Then her voice changed to a new note of fear. "Kup-kup-kup!" she stuttered, watching Philip warily all the time.

Philip looked closer. He gasped in horror. A piece of thick, rough string was looped twice around the bird's neck. Another piece of string was wound right round her wings, holding them close to her body. Every time she struggled, the string hurt her. She couldn't fly. She couldn't move.

Philip jumped up and banged on the front door.

"Mum!" he called. "Come quick!"

His mother opened the door. She stared at the trembling bird.

"However did that string get round her neck?" she asked.

"There's string round her wings too. Look!" said Philip, pointing. "It couldn't have come there by accident. Someone must have put it there."

"No-one would ever do that, Philip! It's far too cruel!"

Philip knew how to handle a sea-bird. Dad had taught him years ago, on the island. He took off his grey jumper and draped it gently over the gull's head. Then he gripped her firmly around the shoulders and lifted her up, keeping his hands well clear of that fierce yellow beak under the pullover.

"Let me bring her inside, Mum," he said. "We'll have to phone a vet."

Philip lowered the bird to the sofa and held her there, the jumper still covering her head. The dark, warm cloth seemed to calm her, but the cries never stopped.

"Kup-kup-kup-kup!"

Mum shut Jip in the kitchen for a while. Then she found the telephone number of a vet who lived nearby. She talked urgently into the phone, her words falling from her mouth in a fast jumble.

"Sorry," the vet said to Mum with a laugh. "We don't usually come out for wild birds, you know."

"Please!" Mum begged. "Just this once."

"Where do you live?" the vet asked her.

Mum gave him the name of the street and the number of the house.

"Well, it's on my way home. I'll be there in ten minutes."

"Thanks," breathed Mum. She turned to Philip. "He's coming!" she said.

Philip smiled in relief.

The vet had large, kind hands. He knew exactly what to do. First he pulled on a pair of

thick gloves to protect himself from the bird's
sharp beak. Then, very gently, he lifted
Philip's jumper off her head and picked her up.
He held her wings still with one firm hand.
With the other hand, he slowly unwound the
string that was tangled round her neck. Her
pink webbed feet hung limp. They hardly
moved. Then, more carefully still, the vet
unwound the string from her wings. That was
difficult. The string hurt her as he eased it off.
She struggled against his hand and snapped

fiercely at his gloves, but he didn't let go.

Just at that moment, Anna and Ellie came bursting in through the front door.

"School wasn't too bad at all, Mum!" Anna shouted cheerfully. Jip recognised her voice and barked from the kitchen.

"Shh!" whispered Philip. "Don't frighten our herring gull. She's a long way from home."

Ellie froze. Anna was shocked into silence when she saw the string on the floor and the vet with a gull in his hands.

"She'll be all right," said the vet with a smile. "We've caught her before this string had bitten too deep. But she's very tired now. What she needs is a good long rest after a shock like that. She'll fly away in the morning."

"Back to her island," murmured Philip.

"Now, Philip," said the vet, "I'll keep holding her while you get a box ready. She'll need a big cardboard box with lots of holes cut in the lid. Can you find one?"

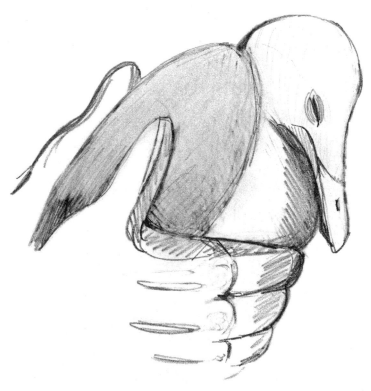

Philip nodded. He ran to his room and tipped all his old treasures out of a large cardboard box. He slashed a few holes in the lid with his penknife and carried the box to the vet.

"That's fine," said the vet. "Now, she'd better get used to your hands, Philip, so I'll hold her beak while you lift her up and put her into the box. That's the way! You'd make a good vet, you know. You've got the knack!"

Philip lowered the trembling bird into the box. He could feel the flutter of her heart through the warm feathers. The vet placed a dish of water next to the bird. Then Philip took his hands gently from her back. He put the lid on the box again.

"She'll sleep all night now," said the vet. "Tomorrow morning, first pull on some thick gloves. Then lift the gull out and keep holding her gently while you give her a bowl of tinned dog-food and a fresh dish of water."

"Dog-food!" Philip laughed out loud in amazement.

"She'll love it!" said the vet. "That'll be enough to keep her going all through the day while she's flying."

"But where will she stop for the next night?" Anna asked anxiously.

"She'll spy a pond in a park or a wood and down she'll come! " said the vet. "The day after that, she'll probably fly straight to the sea."

"And to the island!" said Philip. "We've often seen herring gulls on our island."

"What island's that?" asked the vet, his eyes lighting up with interest.

"Benbecula!" Philip said proudly.

"The best island in the whole world," said Ellie.

"I've been there myself!" said the vet, smiling at them all. "A great place for sea-birds!"

Philip smiled back at him. "So in the morning, when she's had her dog-food and her drink of water, what do I do then?" he asked.

"Just let her fly!" said the vet. He waved and was gone.

The next morning, Philip pulled on his dad's old driving gloves. They were a bit too big for him. He lifted up the bird and poked her beak into the dish of dog-food. She gobbled up a few hungry mouthfuls and she sipped eagerly at the water. Then Philip carried her out to the

back garden. He held her high in his hands.
He threw her into the air. She flew!

The whole family stood with Philip and
watched the bird as she climbed high into the
air. Then she pointed her head towards the
sea and flew steadily out of their sight.

"She's off to her island!" Philip said
wistfully. "One day *I'll* go back too!"